Miracle·Gro®

Vegetables

How to grow fresh, delicious vegetables

Table of Contents

Meredith® Books
Des Moines, Iowa

Miracle-Gro Basics – Vegetables
Writer: Megan McConnell Hughes
Editor: Marilyn Rogers
Contributing Designer: Studio G Design
Copy Chief: Terri Fredrickson
Publishing Operations Manager: Karen Schirm
Senior Editor, Asset and Information Manager: Phillip Morgan
Edit and Design Production Coordinator: Mary Lee Gavin
Editorial Assistant: Kathleen Stevens
Book Production Managers: Pam Kvitne, Marjorie J. Schenkelberg, Rick von Holdt, Mark Weaver
Contributing Copy Editor: Sara Oliver Watson
Contributing Proofreaders: Terri Krueger, Stephanie Petersen
Contributing Photographers: Bill Beatty/Wild & Natural: 29B; Rob Cardillo: 43T; David
  Cavagnaro: 22TR, 26CR, 26BR, 28CR, 28BR, 30BR, 32TR, 32BR, 33T, 33B, 34CR, 34BR,
  38TR, 38BR, 40TR; Jerry Pavia: 22BR, 32L, 33corner, 34TR, 38L, 38CR, 40L, 40CR, 40BR,
  41corner; Michael Thompson: 28TR
Contributing Photo Researcher: Susan Ferguson
Contributing Photo Stylist: Diane Witosky
Indexer: Elizabeth T. Parson
Special thanks to: Janet Anderson, Mary Irene Swartz

Meredith Books
Executive Director, Editorial: Gregory H. Kayko
Executive Director, Design: Matt Strelecki
Managing Editor: Amy Tincher-Durik
Executive Editor/Group Manager: Benjamin W. Allen
Senior Associate Design Director: Ken Carlson
Marketing Product Manager: Isaac Petersen

Publisher and Editor in Chief: James D. Blume
Editorial Director: Linda Raglan Cunningham
Executive Director, New Business Development: Todd M. Davis
Executive Director, Sales: Ken Zagor
Director, Operations: George A. Susral
Director, Production: Douglas M. Johnston
Director, Marketing: Amy Nichols
Business Director: Jim Leonard

Vice President and General Manager: Douglas J. Guendel

Meredith Publishing Group
President: Jack Griffin
Executive Vice President: Bob Mate

Meredith Corporation
Chairman and Chief Executive Officer: William T. Kerr
President and Chief Operating Officer: Stephen M. Lacy

In Memoriam: E.T. Meredith III (1933-2003)

All of us at Meredith₀ Books are dedicated to providing you with information and ideas to
enhance your home and garden. We welcome your comments and suggestions. Write to us at:
Meredith Books, Garden Editorial Department, 1716 Locust St., Des Moines, IA 50309-3023.

If you would like more information on other Miracle-Gro products, call 800/225-2883 or visit us
at: www.miraclegro.com

Note to the Readers: Due to differing conditions, tools, and individual skills, Meredith
Corporation assumes no responsibility for any damages, injuries suffered, or losses incurred as a
result of following the information published in this book. Before beginning any project, review the
instructions carefully, and if any doubts or questions remain, consult local experts or authorities.

Excerpted from Miracle-Gro Basics, *Vegetables*, © 2006, ISBN 0-696-22568-9

Fresh from the Garden

Fresh is best! Here's one of many reasons why. A fresh-picked, vine-ripened tomato has up to three times the vitamin C of a supermarket tomato, and the flavor is so rich and delicious it's hard to believe that the two are related. Ultimate freshness and fabulous flavor are at your fingertips in a home vegetable garden. When the distance from the garden to the table is mere feet, you'll enjoy just-harvested, nutrient-packed produce that is superior to any store-bought counterpart because it is so fresh.

A well-stocked vegetable garden doesn't require a huge planting patch. In fact, you can grow a great selection of vegetables in containers on a sunny deck or patio. Dedicate a few minutes a day to weeding, watering, and harvesting vegetables and you'll enjoy weeks of good-for-you treats.

< 3 >

HOW TO USE THIS BOOK
Plant Selection Guide

Flip to the Gallery of Vegetables beginning on page 21 to learn about growing 10 different vegetables. Each plant summary includes several recommended varieties and helpful growing tips.

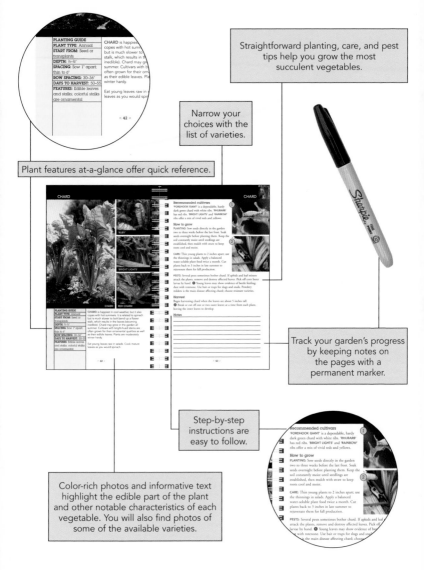

Straightforward planting, care, and pest tips help you grow the most succulent vegetables.

Narrow your choices with the list of varieties.

Plant features at-a-glance offer quick reference.

Track your garden's progress by keeping notes on the pages with a permanent marker.

Step-by-step instructions are easy to follow.

Color-rich photos and informative text highlight the edible part of the plant and other notable characteristics of each vegetable. You will also find photos of some of the available varieties.

Recommended cultivars
'FORDHOOK GIANT' is a dependable, hardy dark green chard with white ribs. 'RHUBARB' has red ribs. 'BRIGHT LIGHTS' and 'RAINBOW' ribs offer a mix of vivid reds and yellows.

How to grow
PLANTING: Sow seeds directly in the garden two to three weeks before the last frost. Soak seeds overnight before planting them. Keep the soil constantly moist until seedlings are established, then mulch with straw to keep roots cool and moist.

CARE: Thin young plants to 2 inches apart; use the thinnings in salads. Apply a balanced water-soluble plant food twice a month. Cut plants back to 3 inches in late summer to rejuvenate them for fall production.

PESTS: Several pests sometimes bother chard. If aphids and leaf miners attack the plants, remove and destroy affected leaves. Pick off corn borer larvae by hand. Young leaves may show evidence of beetle feeding; dust with rotenone. Use bait or traps for slugs and snails. Powdery mildew is the main disease affecting chard; choose resistant varieties.

< 4 >

Vegetables are an easy-to-please lot. They grow with gusto on apartment balconies, ripen happily when mixed with flowers in beds of annuals and perennials, and turn out mouthwatering produce in traditional backyard gardens.

A successful vegetable garden begins with a good planting site. Although vegetables are adaptable to diverse growing situations, they thrive in the following conditions.

❶ SUNLIGHT: Most vegetables need full sun, which means a daily dose of at least six hours of direct sun. Tomatoes, corn, cucumbers, melons, and potatoes flower and fruit best when they receive sunlight for more than six hours, while salad greens, broccoli, chard, and cabbage can grow well with only four to six hours of direct sunlight.

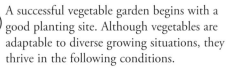

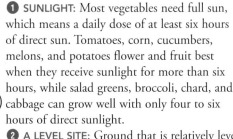

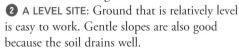

❷ A LEVEL SITE: Ground that is relatively level is easy to work. Gentle slopes are also good because the soil drains well.

❸ DRAINAGE: Soil in a vegetable garden should drain freely. Standing water or persistently soggy soil will inhibit growth and eventually drown plants. You can improve poorly draining soil by incorporating compost into it. Or you can create raised beds. Building a 6- to 12-inch-tall frame and filling it with good quality topsoil will raise the root system above the poorly drained native soil.

For convenience, site a vegetable garden close to the kitchen door. Running out at dinnertime to harvest some parsley or one more tomato for the salad will be a cinch. You'll also find it's handy to locate the garden near a shed or garage where tools can be stored. A nearby water source will make occasional watering chores a snap.

< 6 >

Traditional vegetable gardens are planted in straight rows to make tilling, hoeing, and harvesting a breeze. They're functional spaces and they look it. Plant them in an out-of-the-way space in the landscape so they are not an eyesore. ❹ If you select a planting site that is visible from a living area, there are many ways to make the garden eye-pleasing. For example, surround it with a tidy picket fence, install brick paths between raised beds, or mix in flowers for color.

If space is limited, plant vegetables in containers. Bush or patio tomatoes, peppers, eggplant, and lettuce are good crops for container gardens. Grow lettuce in 6- to 10-inch-diameter pots; containers holding 5 to 15 gallons of soil are best for larger plants. Be sure the pots have adequate drainage holes to allow excess water to escape. Fill the containers with Miracle-Gro Potting Mix and plant seeds or transplants.

< 7 >

Soil Preparation

Vegetables thrive and taste better if they grow in good soil. The best soil for vegetable gardening is loose, crumbly, and dark, which means the soil has plenty of organic matter. Good soil for vegetable gardens contains necessary nutrients for plant growth and is free of weed seeds and pesticide residue. If your garden plot is not blessed with great soil, don't worry. As you prepare for planting, you can improve the soil.

Fall is the ideal time to prepare garden soil. ① Extended dry spells this time of year make the soil easy to turn over. Plus, when you amend the soil in fall, the earthworms and microorganisms in the soil have time to process the organic matter you add, so that its nutrients are available to plants by springtime.

If you don't get a chance to work the soil in fall, prepare it anytime it is dry and crumbly. Soil preparation requires time, labor, and monetary investment, but it pays dividends in bushels of flavorful vegetables. Prepare your planting area with these simple steps.

Determine the size and shape of the garden. ② If this is your first garden, it is best to start small. The largest size recommended for a first vegetable garden is 25 by 25 feet—625 square feet. With careful planning, a garden this size can keep four people supplied with loads of salad makings, herbs, and vegetables.

Once you determine the size of your garden, design the shape of the space. Traditional row-crop gardens are rectangular. If you want a more decorative garden, shape it with gentle sweeping curves. ❶ Outline the bed with markers or a garden hose. Once you are happy with the shape, mark it with sand, flour, or landscapers paint, then remove the hose.

❷ Remove sod and weeds. If you are making the garden in a spot that is currently lawn, use

< 8 >

a sharp spade to strip the grass off of the area. Use the sod elsewhere or compost it. If you are removing sod from a large area, consider renting a power sod cutter.

3 Spread 4 inches of organic material over the bed. Use Miracle-Gro Garden Soil, decomposed bark chips or manure, compost, leaf mold, sphagnum peat moss, or a combination of these materials. Organic matter improves drainage and air circulation in the soil, while boosting its nutrient content. Vegetables will utilize these valuable nutrients as they grow.

4 Use a rotary tiller to churn it all into the soil. Owning a tiller is not necessary; garden centers and hardware stores rent rotary tillers at reasonable rates. Tillers with large wheels are the easiest to operate. If the soil is heavy and hard to dig, rent the largest tiller you can find. The weight and power make the job easier.

Once the garden spot is bare, water the area and then let it rest for a few days. Treat any weeds that pop up with Roundup Weed & Grass Killer. Roundup breaks down in the soil in a few days and has no effect on the vegetables to follow. Repeat the process in 10 days to kill any new weeds that germinate. Wait another 10 days to see whether you need to spray again.

5 Prepare the seed or transplant bed. Rake the area smooth and discard any rocks, sticks, clods, or other debris. Spread plant food according to label directions. Use a continuous release or organic formulation to last all summer. Rake the plant food into the soil and water it in, and you're ready to plant.

< **9** >

Starting From Seed

The plants for your vegetable garden start either as seeds you sow yourself—inside or in the garden—or as transplants that you buy. Garden centers and mail order companies boast a diverse selection of seeds and seedlings. Growing vegetable transplants at home from seed is an economical choice, but you must be willing to provide regular care to ensure the small plants thrive.

Starting vegetables from seed is an excellent option if you would like to grow a particular variety or heirloom that is not sold as a transplant. Some vegetables, such as corn, beans, peas, and lettuce, are so simple to sow directly into the garden that you rarely find them as transplants. Many others, such as artichoke, celery, eggplant, pepper, and tomato, need a long growing season to mature. Usually nurseries offer these vegetables as transplants, but you can also start your own transplants at home. Sow them indoors in late winter and move them into the garden in late spring.

Seed packets clearly explain when and how to plant for your particular area of the country. Grow your own transplants with these tips.

❶ CONTAINERS: Nearly any container, from peat pots to egg cartons, can be used for sowing seed. The only requirement is that water can drain out of the pot.

❷ SOIL: Seed-starting soil mix, such as Miracle-Gro Seed Starting Potting Mix, is best for starting seedlings.
SOWING: Fill containers with moist soil mix, water well, and let drain. Plant seeds as recommended on the seed packet.

❸ WATERING: Water seeds and seedlings delicately with a slow stream of water or by misting them. Keep the soil moist.

< 10 >

LIGHT AND HEAT: Seedlings need plenty of light  to develop into strong plants, and a sunny windowsill doesn't provide enough. Growing seedlings on a light stand equipped with fluorescent grow lamps is the best way to meet your seedlings' needs. Adjust the lamps so they are 2 inches above the plants, raising the lamps as the plants grow. Keep the lights on for 12 to 14 hours per day.

Most vegetables will sprout at room temperature (about 70°F), but some plants, such as peppers, cabbages, and tomatoes, will germinate much faster if given slightly warmer temperatures. To increase warmth, place the containers on a heating pad set on its lowest temperature. Shut off the pad at night. Keep seeds moist, warm, and exposed to adequate light until they germinate. Seeds will germinate in a few days to a few weeks, depending on the plant species.

❹ **THINNING:** Seedlings typically first unfold two small, delicate leaves, called seed leaves. The next leaves to appear are the "true" leaves. These are usually larger and have a different shape. When plants are about 1 inch tall and before the first true leaves develop, remove all but the strongest seedlings in the pot. You can pull out the excess plants or pinch or clip off the stems at soil level.

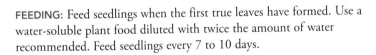

FEEDING: Feed seedlings when the first true leaves have formed. Use a water-soluble plant food diluted with twice the amount of water recommended. Feed seedlings every 7 to 10 days.

❺ **HARDENING OFF:** Prepare seedlings for the outdoors by hardening them off. During this phase, you toughen up seedlings by exposing them to cooler temperatures, letting their soil dry so they wilt slightly, and giving them more light. An easy way to harden off seedlings is to set them outside in mild weather for two or three weeks before planting them in the garden. Keep the seedlings out of strong wind and bring them indoors if frost is expected.

< 11 >

Into the Garden

Vegetables fall into two groups—warm-season and cool-season crops—and you need to know which group a vegetable is in so that you plant it in the garden at the right time.

Cool-season crops, such as lettuce and cabbage, thrive when temperatures range between 40°F and 75°F. In most areas, plant cool-season crops two to four weeks before the last average spring frost date. They will stop producing in early summer when the weather warms.

Warm-season vegetables, such as tomatoes, peppers, and corn, are killed by frost and don't germinate or perform well when temperatures fall below 50°F. Plant warm-season crops in the garden after the last chance of frost has passed. See the list of warm- and cool-season crops on page 13.

Planting

1 Once the time is right for planting outdoors, make sure the soil is ready. It should be neither too wet nor too dry. Press a handful of soil in your fist; if it crumbles, the soil is ready. Before planting, loosen the soil by tilling or turning it with a long-handled garden fork. Smooth over the bed with a rake, breaking up large clods and making sure the soil surface is finely textured.

Sowing seeds

2 Begin by digging a shallow furrow with a hoe or trowel. Drop seeds into the furrow, placing them as close together as recommended on the seed packet. Cover small seeds such as lettuce and carrots with a scant 1/4 inch of soil; cover larger seeds such as corn and beans with an inch or more or simply press them into the ground. Check the seed-packet recommendations for planting depth.

Gently water the garden as soon as seeds are sown; soil should be moist but not wet. Some seeds germinate in a few days while others take three weeks or more to send up shoots.

< **12** >

3 When seedlings reach 1 to 2 inches in height, thin them to the spacing recommended on the seed packet.

Establishing transplants

If buying transplants, select young, healthy seedlings with strong stems and vivid green foliage. To plant, gently loosen pot-bound roots—the ones tightly encircling the root ball—so they don't continue to grow around themselves. Then plant at the same depth as the seedling grew in the pot.

Plant tomato and broccoli seedlings deeper so they don't flop over. They'll actually grow roots on the buried stem, which helps stabilize them. Water well.

Extend the season

4 The sooner you get plants into the garden the better they will grow and the sooner they will produce fruit. Cold weather and soil often inhibit early outdoor planting. Get a jump-start on the season by using bottom-less, gallon-size plastic milk jugs to make mini greenhouses. Be sure to remove the jugs when temperatures rise above 50°F; otherwise the plants might "cook" underneath. Cold frames, plastic tunnels, and row covers also work to warm soil for good plant growth.

Warm-season crops	Cool-season crops
SOW IN WARM SOIL: Beans Cantaloupe Corn Cucumber Okra Pumpkin Squash Watermelon **TRANSPLANT TO GARDEN IN LATE SPRING:** Artichoke Eggplant Pepper Tomato	**SOW IN COOL SOIL:** Arugula Beet Broccoli Cabbage Carrot Chard Kohlrabi Lettuce Onion Parsnip Peas Potato Radish Spinach

Garden Care

To reach their fullest potential, vegetables have to grow as quickly as possible. Anything that slows growth decreases the size and the quality of the produce, as well as the yield. Regular watering, feeding, and other care give plants the oomph they need to grow quickly and produce a tasty, bountiful harvest.

Watering

Water is most important for taste and yield. Give vegetables all the water they want and don't let them go through periods of drought. The most critical time to water is right after seeds are sown or seedlings planted. Without moisture, seeds will not germinate. And a transplant plunked down into dry soil droops very quickly. Water a just-seeded bed with a fine shower of water right after planting, then as needed to maintain a moist but not wet seedbed. Water transplants immediately after planting and continue as needed to create moist but not waterlogged soil.

As plants grow, water as needed based on the feel of the soil an inch or so under the surface. When it feels cool and damp to the touch, but doesn't moisten your finger, it's time to water; if it wets or muddies your finger, it's too soon to water; if it feels dry, you've waited too long.

Each time you water, let the hose run until the soil is wet a foot below the surface. To determine whether you've applied enough water without digging, set soup cans around the garden to measure the amount of water you're applying. For average soils, an inch of water in the can equals 12 inches deep in the soil. Clay soils might need 2 inches, and sandy soils only half an inch.

< 14 >

1 Soaker hoses, with small holes that slowly emit water, are an efficient and effective way to water a vegetable garden. Avoid overhead watering methods, such as sprinklers and watering cans, which wet foliage and promote disease growth.

Feeding

Vegetables have a voracious appetite for nutrients. In fact, vegetables require more nutrients than any other plants in the garden.

Different plant foods are applied in different ways. Follow the directions on the box or bag for application and timing.

2 Watch your plants. If growth slows or the oldest leaves begin to turn yellow, give a quick feeding of liquid plant food on the leaves and the soil. Another way to give plants a quick boost is to side-dress them with a quick-release granular plant food. **3** Scratch the food into the base of the plant or along the row. Then water it in to prevent burning.

FEEDING TIPS: Get transplants off to a growing start in the garden with the following formula. At planting time mix Osmocote Smart-Release Plant Food in the planting holes as directed on the package. This plant food will slowly release valuable nutrients throughout the growing season. After planting the transplants feed them with Miracle-Gro All Purpose fertilizer for a quick nutrient boost. Follow-up with another application of Miracle-Gro All Purpose fertilizer two weeks later.

Vegetables in containers need more food than those in the ground. A regular liquid-feeding schedule works well with them. An excellent way to feed vegetables in dry climates is to add some plant food to the irrigation water. Add one-fourth the recommended rate every time you water. Water after feeding to dissolve the plant food and carry it into the root zone. You can take care of both by using a water-soluble plant food that feeds as you water.

Weed Control

Weeds compete with vegetables for water, sun, and soil nutrients. If you ignore the weeds, they will reduce your harvest. Attack weeds before they grow large. Use one or, better still, a combination of the following methods to defeat weeds in your garden.

continued on page 16>>

< 15 >

1 MULCH: Mulch smothers weed seeds and makes weeds easier to pull if they do germinate and grow. Spread a 2-inch layer of organic mulch, such as straw, grass clippings, compost, or shredded leaves, around plants. Synthetic mulches, such as plastic mulch—available in several colors—and fiber weed cloth, are also good at suppressing pesky weeds.

2 HOEING: If you don't mulch, hoeing and cultivating the soil is another way to control weeds. Hoeing also loosens any crust that forms on soil, which can prevent water from entering and filtering down to the plant roots. Work only the top inch of soil, hoeing lightly every few days.

HAND WEEDING: Weeds are easiest to remove from moist earth, so hand weed after rain or watering. Pull the weed out by its roots. Use a trowel or dandelion digger to eradicate weeds with long taproots.

3 HERBICIDES: Most herbicides are formulated to kill specific types of plants. When buying, read the label to make sure the product can be used safely on your crops. Apply herbicides with care to avoid damaging plants or the environment. Weed preventers, such as Miracle-Gro Garden Weed Preventer, are formulated to keep weeds from germinating then growing in your garden. They work best if they are applied early in the season. Before using a weed preventer, remove any weeds that have broken through the soil.

Harvest

4 Vegetables are best when picked when flavor is at its peak. This means harvesting the crovps when they are ready and not leaving fruit on the plant too long. Cucumbers, for example,

< 16 >

become coarse and full of seeds if not picked promptly. Also, harvesting vegetables is like picking flowers; the plants stop producing if the crops are not harvested.

Seed packets and plant catalogs usually list "days to harvest" to give you an idea of when the crop will be ready to pick. Some crops, such as radishes, are ready for harvest in 25 to 30 days; other crops take 90 days or more to mature.

Take note of the days to harvest for your crops and time planting in your garden accordingly. For example, if you will be away from your garden for two weeks in August, expedite or delay planting vegetables so that they fruit before you leave or after you return. By doing this you'll enjoy all the fruit of your labor at its peak.

For harvesting purposes, vegetable crops can be divided into three categories: those that should be harvested as soon as they are ripe, those that can wait a few days, and those that can wait a few weeks. For ultimate flavor, pick vegetables as recommended below.

HARVEST AS SOON AS THEY RIPEN: beans, corn, cucumbers, and peas.
HARVEST WITHIN A FEW DAYS AFTER RIPENING: broccoli, cabbage, lettuce, radishes, summer squash, tomatoes, and zucchini.
CAN LEAVE IN THE GARDEN FOR SEVERAL WEEKS: beets and other root vegetables, carrots, kale, leeks, pumpkins, winter squash.

< 17 >

Sometimes, in spite of our best efforts, things go wrong. Weeds, pests, diseases, or environmental problems, such as too little light or too much water, plague crops and reduce harvest.

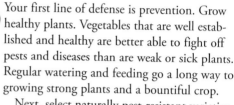

Your first line of defense is prevention. Grow healthy plants. Vegetables that are well established and healthy are better able to fight off pests and diseases than are weak or sick plants. Regular watering and feeding go a long way to growing strong plants and a bountiful crop.

Next, select naturally pest-resistant varieties. Numerous vegetable varieties are resistant to specific problems. For example, the ears of some corn cultivars are so tightly wrapped in the husk that corn earworms can't reach them. Some tomato varieties resist a range of diseases.

Finally, if you know that a particular pest is an ongoing and serious problem in your area, either search for resistant varieties or don't grow that vegetable at all.

Pest Control

The Gallery of Vegetables, which starts on page 21, points out the most notorious pests of each vegetable. For more information about your problem, see The Ortho Problem Solver. This reference guide includes pictures of many vegetable problems and specific information on how to control the pest.

Insects

Vigilance is the best way to control insect pests. Watch for signs of insect problems and nip them in the bud as soon as they appear. A few aphids are much easier to deal with than thousands of them. ❶ Start with the least-toxic pest control strategy, such as row covers or barriers, to exclude pests from crops altogether. ❷ When pest populations are low, handpick insects and drop them into soapy

< 18 >

water to kill them. Reach for pesticides when the pest is clearly out of control and an important crop is at risk. Be sure to select a pesticide that will control the specific pest infesting your crop.

Diseases

Sometimes correcting environmental conditions can control vegetable diseases without the need for fungicides. For example, you can prevent the spread of fungal diseases by watering with a drip hose to avoid getting foliage wet. Rotating crops, such as planting tomatoes in a new spot every year, will prevent soilborne diseases.

Weeds

❸ Like insects, weeds are best controlled with vigilance. Create conditions that favor the vegetables and suppress the weeds, then be on the lookout for interlopers and get rid of them before they set seed.

< 19 >

Prepare for Winter

As crop production wanes in early fall, it's time to clean up the garden and prepare it for winter. A debris-free garden will be quick and easy to prepare for planting in spring and it will be less likely to harbor pests and diseases from the previous season. Prepare your planting plot for winter with these tips.

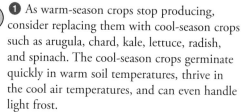

1 As warm-season crops stop producing, consider replacing them with cool-season crops such as arugula, chard, kale, lettuce, radish, and spinach. The cool-season crops germinate quickly in warm soil temperatures, thrive in the cool air temperatures, and can even handle light frost.

2 When plants die, remove them from the garden. Dead plants provide a home where pests and diseases overwinter. Pull plants up by the roots and throw them into the compost heap. If plants were diseased or plagued by insects, throw them into the trash to avoid spreading problems.

3 In late fall, turn under any old mulch and dig out weeds. If soil is dry enough for tilling, incorporate a 3- to 4-inch layer of decomposed organic matter, such as compost, into the soil.

< 20 >

'KENTUCKY WONDER' POLE BEAN

LIMA BEAN

FAVA BEAN

POLE BEANS

PLANTING GUIDE	
PLANT TYPE: Annual	
START FROM: Seed	
DEPTH: 1"	
SPACING: Sow 2–3" apart; thin to 6"	
ROW SPACING: 24–36"	
DAYS TO HARVEST: 40–100	
FEATURES: Edible seeds and immature pods; easy-to-grow crop	

BEANS are a favorite vegetable of new and experienced gardeners alike. All beans need full sun and well-drained soil and, except for favas, are warm-weather crops, easily damaged by frost. They are a diverse crop. Some varieties boast colorful flowers and fruit, while others scramble up trellises; they are as pretty as they are productive. Some varieties bear both edible pods and seeds and others just edible seeds.

Bush beans, the most popular for home gardens, are excellent producers. Once the plants start producing, you'll get several quick crops in two or three weeks.

< 22 >

Recommended species and cultivars

BUSH BEANS are the most common bean in home gardens. They grow knee-high and produce edible pods about 60 days after sowing. Sow seeds after the last frost and make several small sowings three weeks apart for a long harvest. There are several types of bush beans.

SNAP BEANS have round or flat pods that vary in color from green to yellow to purple. They are your standard green bean. Harvest snap beans when the pods begin to fill out. 'VENTURE', 'DERBY', and 'PROVIDER' are among the many dependable varieties of snap beans.

SHELL BEANS can be eaten as green snap beans; harvest when pods are young and tender. Or you can let the beans ripen until the seeds become plump and the pods feel leathery. Harvest the beans before they actually dry. Shell the beans before cooking and eating. **LIMA BEANS** fall into this category. They tolerate heat, humidity, and insects and diseases. Harvest limas when the pods are plump but still glossy. Limas can be eaten fresh, frozen, or preserved as dry beans. Fast-maturing limas, such as 'FORDHOOK 242', will grow in northern gardens, but other lima cultivars are most productive in areas with long summers.

DRY SHELL BEANS are similar to shell beans but are usually eaten dried. Red kidney, pinto, and black beans are examples. Allow dry beans to ripen on the plants until the pods turn brown and the plants begin to die. To harvest, pull up the plants

POLE BEANS are similar to bush beans, with one exception. They climb. Pods come in many shapes and colors. As with bush beans, there are snap, shell, and dry beans. To keep plants productive for a long time, promptly pick young pods before they develop large seeds. For pole beans with deep green pods and a long harvest, consider 'KENTUCKY BLUE', 'KENTUCKY WONDER', and 'ROMANO'.

FAVA BEANS require cool weather and can survive temperatures as low as 10°F to 20°F. Plants are large and upright, growing to 5 feet tall. Plant fava beans in fall in climates with mild winters or in spring where summers are cool. Protein-rich fava beans are best harvested while pods are still green. Dry them for a week in a hot place, then crack open the pods. 'BROAD WINDSOR' has excellent flavor.

Notes

_____

_____

_____

_____

BUSH BEANS

How to grow

PLANTING: **①** Direct-sow seeds after all danger of spring frost has passed. In areas with very short growing seasons, give beans an early start by starting seeds indoors several weeks before the last frost date. To save space, you can interplant beans with corn, sweet potatoes, and tomatoes. **②** When plants are a few inches tall, thin them to 6 inches apart.

To create a tripod for supporting pole beans, you'll need three 6- to 8-foot-long poles. Firmly anchor the poles in the ground, tie their tops together, then sow four to six seeds at the base of each pole.

< 24 >

CARE: Beans do best when daytime temperatures are 70°F to 80°F. When temperatures rise above 85°F flowers may drop; plants are also sensitive to frost.

To encourage branching, which increases yield, cut off the tip of each pole bean vine when it gets to the top of the tripod. To hold bush plants off the soil, set stakes at the ends of each row on both sides. Tie string to the stakes 5 inches above the ground.

Bean plants are tender and easily damaged by garden tools, so weed around them by hand. Keep the soil consistently moist; water only in the morning so the plants dry quickly, which reduces the potential for disease.

Beans supply their own nitrogen but benefit from a monthly application of soluble plant food high in phosphorus and potassium.

PESTS: Beans are susceptible to several bacterial and viral diseases. Choose resistant cultivars. Fungal diseases, such as blight, rot, rust, and anthracnose, can also be a problem. Do not plant beans in the same soil year after year; instead, rotate the planting area with other vegetable crops.

The Mexican bean beetle is the main insect pest in home gardens; it lays its eggs on the undersides of bean leaves. Handpick and destroy eggs and larvae, or use neem oil for heavy infestations.

Avoid using insecticides on beans. Bean flowers attract beneficial ladybugs and predatory wasps and are pollinated by bumblebees.

Harvest

❸ Harvest by pinching or cutting pods off the plant. See page 23 for specifics for each type of bean.

Notes

< 25 >

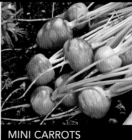

MINI CARROTS

'CHANTENAY'

CARROTS

'SWEETNESS'

PLANTING GUIDE	
PLANT TYPE: Annual	
START FROM: Seed	
DEPTH: ¼–½"	
SPACING: Sow 1" apart; thin to 3–4"	
ROW SPACING: 12–15"	
DAYS TO HARVEST: 50–100	
FEATURES: Edible taproots and leaves; many cultivars available	

CARROTS harvested from the home garden are remarkably crisp and juicy and much more flavorful than their store-bought counterparts. Carrots grow in a wide variety of colors, shapes, and sizes. Miniature carrots that form either round roots or short blunt, cylindrical roots are good for clay soils or containers. Traditional carrots, with their large taproots, grow best in finely textured soil.

Interplant carrots among lettuces, beans, peas, tomatoes, and peppers. They grow well in raised beds. Carrots grow best in cool weather. In many areas, crops sown in the fall can be harvested through winter.

< 26 >

Recommended cultivars

'KINKO' is a 4-inch mini carrot ready to harvest in 50 to 55 days. 'ROUND ROMEO' is a smooth-skinned mini about 1 to 1½ inches in diameter. Short, early carrots ready in 65 to 70 days include 'DANVERS HALF LONG', 'SCARLET NANTES', and 'CHANTENAY'. Large carrots that are good fresh or stored, 'TENDERSWEET', 'SUGARSNAX', 'SWEETNESS', and 'BOLERO', are ready to harvest in 70 to 80 days.

How to grow

PLANTING: Carrots grow best in loose, sandy loam. Direct-sow seed two to four weeks before the last spring frost date. Moisten the soil beforehand so that the tiny seeds don't blow away. Cover seeds with ¼ inch of fine soil and water gently to avoid disturbing the seeds. In areas with long, mild autumns, you can plant a second crop in late summer.

CARE: Keep seeds evenly moist to ensure germination, which can take up to three weeks. ❶ Thin seedlings to about 3 inches apart. Weed carefully with a hoe or pull weeds by hand. Use straw or another organic mulch between rows to retain moisture and minimize weeds, but keep it off the leafy tops.

You can harvest fall-sown carrots all winter. ❷ Cut off the green tops to about an inch and mulch plants heavily with straw. In areas with extreme winters, also place a cold frame over them.

PESTS: No significant pests in the home garden.

Harvest

Begin pulling carrots as soon as their shoulders poke out of the ground and begin to develop color. This is a good way to thin rows to give the remaining carrots a chance to grow larger. In northern zones, wait until the ground has begun to freeze before digging the rest of the carrots; cold weather increases their sweet flavor.

Notes

'BURPLESS BUSH'

'MARKETMORE 97'

VINING CUCUMBER PLANT

'FANCIPAK' PICKLING

PLANTING GUIDE	
PLANT TYPE: Annual	
START FROM: Seed	
DEPTH: ½"	
SPACING: Sow 12" apart; thin to 24"	
ROW SPACING: 5–6'	
DAYS TO HARVEST: 50–70	
FEATURES: Edible fruit; vigorous grower and producer	

CUCUMBERS are easy to grow and often produce more fruit than most gardeners can use. Limit the size of plantings unless you plan to make lots of pickles. Six plants of any type provide plenty of fruit to eat and share. Cucumbers are available in bush or vining types. Bush cukes are compact plants, ideal for containers. Vining types will crawl across the ground or with training will climb a trellis.

For pickling, grow small-fruited pickling cucumbers that produce dozens of small fruit all at once. Slicing cukes have straight fruit. Burpless varieties have thin, tender skin, which makes them easy to digest.

< 28 >

Recommended cultivars

PICKLING: 'LITTLE LEAF' sets fruit without pollination and yields well even during dry spells. 'NORTHERN PICKLING' produces fruit in 45 to 50 days. 'FANCIPAK' is a disease-resistant heirloom variety.

SLICING: 'MARKETMORE' and 'GENERAL LEE' cultivars are popular types. 'DIVA' is an award-winning seedless type that cucumber beetles don't seem to like.

How to grow

PLANTING: Before planting, incorporate generous amounts of compost or other organic matter into the soil. ❶ Direct-sow seed when soil and air temperatures reach at least 60°F. Plant cucumbers in rows or hills of five to seven seeds. Or plant nursery-grown transplants after the last average frost date.

CARE: Thin to three plants per hill or to 6 to 9 inches apart in rows. Keep the soil continuously moist, giving plants at least ½ inch of water per week. Increase watering during periods of high heat. Use row covers to protect young plants from pests and cold. Even a light frost will kill cucumbers. For vining types, install trellises or other supports.

PESTS: Cucumbers are susceptible to many problems. ❷ Cucumber beetles are the most significant pests; they spread bacterial wilt. Pick off and destroy any you find. New hybrids have been developed for disease resistance. Choose cultivars that have been bred specifically for your climate. Use insecticides and fungicides when problems get out of hand. Follow label directions and pay particular attention to timing to avoid killing pollinators.

Harvest

Harvest slicing varieties when they are 8 to 12 inches long and pickling types when 2 inches or longer. Picking frequently increases production; pick daily to prevent fruits from becoming too large.

Notes

_____

_____

_____

< 29 >

MELONS REQUIRE LOTS OF ROOM

'CHARENTAIS' CANTALOUPE

MUSKMELON

'EARLY CRISP' HONEY DEW

PLANTING GUIDE	
PLANT TYPE: Annual	
START FROM: Seed or transplants	
DEPTH: ½"	
SPACING: 2–8'	
ROW SPACING: 5–7'	
DAYS TO HARVEST: 70–100	
FEATURES: Edible fruit; warm-season vining plant	

MELONS are easy to grow in the home garden and often produce several fruits per vine. Space is a consideration when growing melons. Their sprawling vines need about 10 square feet of growing space.

Three types of melons are well-suited to the home garden: true cantaloupes, muskmelons, and winter melons. True cantaloupes have a warty, ribbed rind and sweet, bright-orange flesh. Muskmelons have netted, yellowish rinds and orange flesh. Winter melons vary in appearance. For example, honeydews have a smooth rind and green flesh; crenshaws have yellow rind and salmon-pink flesh.

< 30 >

Recommended cultivars

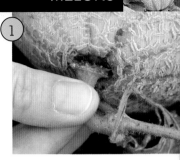

(1)

CANTALOUPE: 'CHARENTAIS' is an early, small melon.

MUSKMELON: 'AMBROSIA' has a small seed cavity and sweet flesh.

WINTER MELON: 'BURPEE'S EARLY HYBRID' is a large yellow-green crenshaw with pink flesh. 'HONEY PEAR' is a medium-size pale gold honeydew that has almost white flesh.

How to grow

PLANTING: Start seeds indoors in peat pots one month before the last frost. One to two weeks after the last frost, move seedlings or purchased transplants to the garden. Or direct-sow five to seven seeds in hills. Thin to two or three seedlings per hill.

CARE: Water consistently, especially while plants are flowering and fruits developing. In dry climates or during periods of drought, provide at least 1 inch of water weekly. Plants need less water when fruit is ripening. Feed at planting, again when fruits begin to form, and about two weeks after fruit-set. Use a low-nitrogen, high-phosphorus, high-potassium plant food.

Protect ripening melons by setting them on inverted pots, boards, or pieces of cardboard. Melons grow best when air temperatures average 70°F. Cool or cloudy weather and too much moisture during fruit development lessen flavor. Provide early-season warmth with plastic tunnels.

PESTS: Striped and spotted cucumber beetles are the worst pests, spreading bacterial wilt; handpick and destroy. Aphids can be troublesome; knock them off with a blast of water. Choose varieties resistant to fusarium wilt, anthracnose, black rot, powdery mildew, and other diseases.

Harvest

Melons ripen from mid- to late summer or early autumn. ❶ Usually, fruit is ripe when the stem easily separates from the fruit. Other clues include deeply colored rind and yellowing or softening at the blossom end of the fruit.

Notes

_____

_____

_____

< 31 >

'MAMBO'

'EARLY YELLOW GLOBE' LONG-DAY ONION   'COPRA'

PLANTING GUIDE	
PLANT TYPE: Annual	
START FROM: Seed, transplants, or dormant bulbs called sets	
DEPTH: ½"	
SPACING: Sow seeds ½"; thin to 3–10"	
ROW SPACING: 12–18"	
DAYS TO HARVEST: 55–300	
FEATURES: Edible bulb and stem	

ONIONS are grown and harvested in many different forms. Cultivate onions for their immature green stems, called scallions; for their young bulbs, called green onions; or for their mature, storable bulbs. Shallots, onions that grow in clusters of 3 to 10 bulbs, are grown for use as dried bulbs and have a delicate flavor.

Choose onions based on their day-length requirements. Short-day varieties do best in warm climates, while long-day cultivars thrive in cool climates. Onions are heavy feeders requiring rich, well-drained soil.

< **32** >

Recommended cultivars

SHORT-DAY VARIETIES: 'YELLOW GRANEX' matures in early summer. 'RED CREOLE' has a pungent flavor. 'NEW MEXICO WHITE GRANO' is a large, mild white onion.

LONG-DAY VARIETIES: 'EARLY YELLOW GLOBE' stores well and is good fresh. 'MAMBO' stores well. 'COPRA' dries quickly for storage.

How to grow

PLANTING: Direct-sow seed in rows a month before the last average frost date. Thin the rows throughout the season, using the thinnings as scallions or green onions.

❶ Plant sets and transplants in early spring in northern areas and in fall in warmer climates. Grow them in rows with the pointed end just showing above ground.

CARE: Water as needed during dry conditions. Weed frequently to reduce competition for nutrients. Remove seed heads, if they form. Mulch to prevent sunscald on bulbs. Use water-soluble plant food twice a month during the growing season.

PESTS: Onions are susceptible to thrips, maggots, and soilborne diseases; to avoid, it's best to plant in a different area each year. Shallots are susceptible to pink rot, particularly in the South; treat soil with fungicide.

Harvest

❷ Dig or pull scallions and green shallots when the tops are 4 to 8 inches tall; green onions are ready when the tops are 6 to 8 inches tall and bulbs have begun to swell. Dig or pull up plants.

If you plan to store onions and shallots, stop watering when the green tops have withered and browned. After a week, dig up shallots; leave onions in the ground for two weeks, then dig them up. Place harvested bulbs in a dry, shady spot for one week. When completely dry, cut off stalks and roots, then hang the bulbs in mesh bags in a cool, dry location.

Notes

_____

_____

_____

< 33 >

'LITTLE MARVEL'

'TALL TELEPHONE'

SHELLING PEAS | 'SUPER SUGAR SNAP'

PLANTING GUIDE

PLANT TYPE: Annual
START FROM: Seed
DEPTH: ½–1"
SPACING: 3–4"
ROW SPACING: 24–48"
DAYS TO HARVEST: 55–75
FEATURES: Edible seeds; some varieties have edible pods

PEAS are a diverse group. Choose among shelling peas—also called garden peas—and edible-pod peas (snap and snow peas). Shell peas are grown for the round seeds within the pods. Snow peas have small peas and sweet pods that stay tender when they mature. They are heavy producers. Snap peas have both full-size seeds and edible pods.

Peas thrive in cool weather. They tolerate brief periods of temperatures below 25°F, but prolonged exposure will interfere with development. Peas are vines that climb by tendrils. There are bush type plants in each group of peas.

< **34** >

Recommended cultivars
Shelling peas

'DAKOTA' is an early variety ready to harvest in 50 to 55 days. Its vines are short enough to be grown without support. 'CASELOAD' is an extra-sweet shelling pea ready in 55 to 60 days. It is slow to become starchy when harvested regularly. 'MAESTRO' and 'ECLIPSE' are good choices for hot southern areas. They are disease resistant and ready in 60 to 65 days. 'ALDERMAN', sometimes called 'TALL TELEPHONE', grows 5 feet or more tall and bears long pods, each with eight to 10 extremely sweet peas in 75 days. It requires a strong support system.

'GREEN ARROW' and 'THOMAS LAXTON' are older varieties that are famous for their rich pea flavor. 'ALASKA' is a short-season variety. It is ready in just 55 days and is good for canning. 'OREGON TRAIL' is ready in 55 to 70 days and is a prolific producer of small pods with sweet peas. It is delicious raw or cooked. 'LITTLE MARVEL' and 'WANDO' are both ready in 60 to 70 days. They tolerate heat well.

Edible-pod peas

SNOW PEAS: 'OREGON GIANT' is a disease-resistant variety that produces sweet, large pods in 60 to 70 days and throughout the summer. 'SUGAR POD 2' is a good choice for cool areas. It is ready to harvest in 60 to 70 days. 'HO LOHN DOW' has large pods and is ready in 60 to 70 days. 'SNOW GREEN' has crisp, flavorful pods.

SNAP PEAS: 'SUGAR ANN' is the earliest snap-pea variety. It is ready to harvest in 50 to 55 days. 'SUGAR SNAP' produces plump, succulent pods in 60 to 70 days in both cool and hot weather. Remove the strings on the pods before eating or cooking them. 'SNAPPY' is sweet and shows some disease resistance. 'SUGAR SPRINT' is a delicious, nearly stringless snap pea. 'SUGAR POP' and 'SUGAR DADDY' are stringless varieties. 'SUPER SUGAR SNAP' is resistant to powdery mildew.

Notes

_____

_____

_____

_____

_____

_____

more about peas > >

< 35 >

BUSH PEAS

How to grow

PLANTING: ❶ Plant peas in early spring in a location where they can be protected from midday sun if temperatures are over 80°F. Grow peas in rich, moist, well-drained soil. Peas do well interplanted with corn, tomatoes, garlic, onions, and lettuce.

CARE: Keep the soil consistently moist and weed by hand to avoid disturbing tender vines and roots. Most peas have weak stems that need support. ❷ A 5-foot trellis made of fence wire, string, or polyester netting will do the job. Or you can support them with pea brush. Save twiggy branches when you prune your shrubs. Poke the cut ends into the soil down the center of the row. Bush types tend to prop up one another well.

< 36 >

PESTS: Peas are susceptible to numerous diseases including leaf spot, scab, blights, rots, fusarium wilt, powdery mildew, botrytis and other molds, damping-off, and mosaic virus. Choose cultivars bred for resistance to bacteria and fungi common in your area. Plant peas in a different area each year to avoid diseases that persist in the soil.

Harvest

❸ Shelling peas are ready to pick when the pea seeds are fully rounded. Store unshelled peas for up to three days and shelled peas for up to seven days. Leave some pods to dry on the vine if you want to keep seed for next year's crop. Pick mature peas regularly for best flavor and to promote the development of other pods.

Harvest snow peas while the pods are still flat and the seeds inside are small and undeveloped.

Pick snap and other edible-pod varieties when the pods are plump and the seeds are fully developed. Store edible-pod peas in the refrigerator for up to one week or blanch and freeze them for up to one year.

Notes

_____

_____

_____

_____

_____

_____

_____

_____

_____

< 37 >

'YUKON GOLD'

'PURPLE PERUVIAN'

POTATO PLANTS

'RED PONTIAC'

PLANTING GUIDE	
PLANT TYPE: Annual	
START FROM: Seed potatoes	
PLANTING DEPTH: 4–6"	
SPACING: 10–12"	
ROW SPACING: 24–36"	
DAYS TO HARVEST: 45–80	
FEATURES: Edible tubers; easy-to-grow, productive plants	

POTATOES are easy to grow and each plant should produce at least five potatoes. Potatoes stop producing new tubers when the soil warms up in summer. For that reason, it is important to choose varieties suited to your climate. In warm climates where the spring season is short, grow only fast-maturing varieties. In areas with long springs, plant both early and midseason potatoes. Small fingerling potatoes are fun to grow in any climate. They produce so many small tubers that you will get a good crop even where the potato season is short.

If your garden space is limited, you can grow potatoes aboveground in large boxes or bins.

< 38 >

Recommended cultivars

Early-maturing varieties ready to harvest in 55 to 75 days include yellow-fleshed 'ADORA', 'CHARLOTTE', and 'YUKON GOLD'; 'PURPLE PERUVIAN', a medium to large fingerling; and 'RED PONTIAC'. 'KENNEBEC' and 'IDA ROSE' are midseason varieties ready in 80 to 90 days. Late-maturing varieties include: 'BUTTE', 'GERMAN BUTTERBALL', and 'NOOKSACK'.

How to grow

PLANTING: Plant seed potatoes two to four weeks before the last frost date. Cut them into pieces, each with one or two eyes, or growing points, and some fleshy tuber attached. Use commercial seed potatoes; grocery store potatoes are usually treated to inhibit sprouting. Dry cut pieces overnight to help prevent rot. ❶ Plant the pieces cut side down in a 4-inch-deep trench in heavy soil or a 6-inch-deep trench in light soil. Cover with 2 to 4 inches of soil.

CARE: Keep soil consistently moist but not waterlogged until plants emerge. Then water only in periods of high heat or drought. Use a plant food that is higher in phosphorus and potassium than in nitrogen, which reduces plant vigor and can lead to disease. Hill soil around the base of the stems when plants are 6 to 8 inches tall, and repeat as they grow taller. When the plants reach full height, top the hills with mulch to conserve moisture and hold weeds down. Cover any tubers poking through the surface with more soil.

PESTS: To avoid blights, remove and destroy vegetative debris where pests may overwinter and plant potatoes in a new area each year. Pick Colorado potato beetles off plants and destroy them.

Harvest

For new potatoes, check plants about a week after they flower. Carefully loosen soil with a garden fork, then reach in to pull up usable size tubers. (Early varieties are the best new potatoes.) Harvest potatoes as needed. For potatoes you plan to store for winter use, leaves tubers in the ground until plant tops die back, then dig up the plants and harvest the potatoes.

Notes

< 39 >

CURLY ENDIVE

ARUGULA

SALAD GREENS   **'MIZUNA' AND ENDIVE**

PLANTING GUIDE	
PLANT TYPE: Annual	
START FROM: Seed	
DEPTH: ¼"	
SPACING: Sow 1" apart; thin to 8–12" apart	
ROW SPACING: 12–24"	
DAYS TO HARVEST: 30–40	
FEATURES: Edible leaves	

SALAD GREENS are easy-to-grow, cool-season crops. They include arugula, endive, mustard, and other spring greens. Arugula is expensive at the grocery but easy to grow. Also known as roquette or rocket, it has a delicious, rich, full-bodied flavor. Endive looks and is planted like leaf lettuce in spring and fall, but it is more cold tolerant. Its flavor is sharp and peppery to almost bitter. Mustards are large, ornamental leafy vegetables with peppery flavor.

A good way to get to know salad greens without buying lots of different seed is to try a mesclun seed blend. Depending on the plants included in the mix, mesclun can be mild, spicy, or bitter.

< 40 >

Recommended cultivars

ARUGULA: 'ASTRO' and 'RUNWAY' are two early, vigorous varieties.

ENDIVE: 'GALIA' is a trouble-free variety with finely cut or curly leaves.

MUSTARD: 'MIZUNA' is an oriental mustard with long feathery leaves. 'RED GIANT' and 'OSAKA PURPLE' are colorful varieties.

How to grow

PLANTING: ❶ Direct-sow salad greens four to six weeks before the last frost. Plant every two weeks for continuous harvest. For fall crops, sow in midsummer in northern regions, late summer to fall in southern areas. ❷ Grow in cold frames for winter harvest.

CARE: Thin seedlings to 8 to 12 inches apart when plants are 3 to 4 inches tall. Water during dry periods. Mulch lightly to suppress weeds; protect plants from intense summer sun with a shade cloth suspended over them with stakes or hoops.

PESTS: Use floating row covers to protect plants from beetles.

Harvest

❸ When arugula and mesclun leaves are about 3 inches long, harvest by cutting handfuls of leaves 1 to 2 inches above the soil surface. Water after harvesting to help plants quickly produce a second crop.

Harvest endive like arugula and mesclun or wait until leaves form a large, loose head with a white to light green heart. Gardeners often blanch mature endive for two weeks before harvest. To blanch, tie outer leaves into a bundle over the hearts; hold it in place with string or a rubber band.

Notes

_____

_____

_____

_____

< 41 >

SUMMER SQUASH

ACORN WINTER SQUASH

PUMPKIN

BUTTERNUT AND OTHER WINTER SQUASHES

PLANTING GUIDE	
PLANT TYPE: Annual	
START FROM: Seed or transplants	
DEPTH: ¾–1"	
SPACING: 18–36"	
ROW SPACING: 72–96"	
DAYS TO HARVEST: 45–120	
FEATURES: Edible fruits	

PUMPKINS AND SQUASH provide fall beauty as well as healthful fruits. Their vigorous vines grow quickly and need as much as 25 square feet to sprawl. For small gardens, look for cultivars that have a compact, bushy habit.

Two groups of vegetables go by the name of squash. Summer squash—including zucchini, Lebanese, pattypan, crookneck, and straightneck—have soft skin. Winter squash—including acorn, butternut, buttercup, hubbard, and pumpkins—have hard, thick rinds, making them suitable for long-term storage.

< 42 >

Recommended cultivars

Hundreds of squash and pumpkin varieties are available. Choose ones suited for your climate.

How to grow

PLANTING: Direct-sow seed two to three weeks after the last spring frost date. Plant in rows or in hills of five to seven seeds. In short-season areas, start seeds indoors four weeks before the last frost date. Move seeds to the garden after the last frost date.

CARE: Squash and pumpkins have high moisture and nutrient requirements. Feed twice a month with water-soluble plant food. Maintain consistently moist but not waterlogged soil. Moisture-stressed plants are more susceptible to insects and diseases and have lower yields. ❶ Because the fruit ripens on the ground, slip a piece of cardboard or another barrier underneath it to prevent rot.

PESTS: ❷ Squash bugs are the most significant pests. Winter squashes are especially susceptible to them. Choose resistant cultivars. Adult squash bugs are difficult to eradicate, so treat plants with Ortho Bug-B-Gon Garden & Landscape Insect Killer when you first see the nymphs. Time sprays carefully to avoid killing pollinators. Crop rotation can also help control insects.

Diseases affecting squash and pumpkins include: fusarium wilt, anthracnose, rots, leaf spots, gummy stem blight, and powdery mildew.

Harvest

Summer squash tastes best when picked small—zucchinis, crooknecks, and straightnecks at about 6 inches long and pattypans at about 3 inches across. Harvest daily when plants are at the height of production.

Winter squash and pumpkins need to mature on the plants until the vines begin to turn yellow and die back; they will not ripen further once picked and do not develop flavor if picked early.

Notes

< 43 >

CHERRY TOMATOES

PLUM TOMATOES

INDETERMINATE TOMATOES

PATIO TOMATOES

PLANTING GUIDE	
PLANT TYPE:	Annual
START FROM:	Seed or transplants
DEPTH:	½"
SPACING:	24–36"
ROW SPACING:	36–72"
DAYS TO HARVEST:	50–80
FEATURES:	Edible fruit

TOMATOES come in diverse sizes, shapes, and colors as well as growing habits. You can purchase plum, cherry, grape, pear, or beefsteak types in red, yellow, peach, black, green, or variegated colors.

Successfully growing tomatoes is simple: Choose disease-resistant varieties suited to your climate and do everything you can to help the plants grow steadily and without interruption.

< **44** >

Recommended cultivars

There are three types of tomatoes: determinate, vigorous determinate, and indeterminate.

DETERMINATE tomatoes, sometimes called dwarf varieties, grow into bushy plants that need no support and develop clusters of blossoms and fruit at the stem tips. They mature early and ripen within one to two weeks, so they are ideal for canning or freezing and for growing in short-season areas. Generally, the fruit ripens over a concentrated period of time, usually three weeks, then the plants die. 'TINY TIM' is a compact plant suitable for containers. 'BUSH EARLY GIRL' is a small, disease-resistant plant that bears large fruit. 'CELEBRITY' is a disease-resistant midseason cultivar with 7- to 8-ounce fruits. 'SHADY LADY' is popular in hot climates. 'SUPER BUSH' bears large, meaty fruit all season but is only 3 feet tall and wide and requires no stakes or cages. 'ROMA' and 'LAROMA' have rich, meaty, almost seedless fruits on compact, disease-resistant vines. 'WINDOWBOX ROMA' is good for growing in containers.

VIGOROUS DETERMINATE tomatoes produce a heavy crop all at once, but they do not die afterward. If you prune them back and fertilize them in midsummer after harvest, vigorous determinates produce a light second crop. They are increasingly popular as double-crop tomatoes, especially in warm climates. 'HUSKY GOLD' is a good yellow-fruiting cultivar.

INDETERMINATE tomatoes produce a summerlong stream of flowers and fruit. The tall, lanky plants require support from stakes, a trellis, or wire cages. Their fruit usually has excellent flavor, and plants remain productive until frost, insects, or diseases kill them. 'GRAPE' is a small, sweet, early, disease-resistant cultivar. 'JOLLY' bears extra-sweet fruits whose tips are pointed like peaches. 'EARLY GIRL' is a popular early slicing tomato that adapts well to almost any climate and is disease resistant. 'SIOUX' is an heirloom variety with exceptional flavor. 'BRANDYWINE' and 'GERMAN JOHNSON' are hybrid heirloom beefsteak varieties with very large dark pink fruit often weighing a pound or more apiece.

Notes

_____

_____

_____

more about tomatoes >>

< 45 >

BEEFSTEAK-TYPE TOMATO

YELLOW PEAR TOMATO

'BRANDYWINE' HEIRLOOM TOMATO

'SUBARCTIC PLENTY'

How to grow

PLANTING: You'll harvest tomatoes sooner by starting with transplants, which you can buy transplants or grow yourself. Sow seeds indoors 6 to 10 weeks before the last frost date. Put the pots in a warm (75°F to 85°F), spot where you can set up grow-lights. Illuminate the seedlings for 12 hours each day, raising the lamps every few days so that they are 3 inches above the tops of the plants.

Plant seedlings in the garden after the last frost date has passed. Dig a deep hole or a trench long enough that you can bury the stem. Place a handful of well-rotted compost in the bottom of the hole or trench, ❶ then set the plant in it. Cover stem and roots with soil, water thoroughly, and apply a starter plant solution. ❷ Stake the plants or set cages over

< 46 >

them now to avoid injuring roots later. Staking elevates foliage so air circulates around it and holds the fruits off the ground, which increases yield. The mesh of cages should be large enough to reach through for harvest. Stakes should be at least 8 feet tall, 1 inch around, and made of sturdy wood or metal. Begin tying stems to the stakes with strips of soft cloth or garden twine when their tips droop.

CARE: Tomatoes need plenty of water to develop juicy fruits and resist disease. Water regularly and apply organic mulch to conserve soil moisture and control weeds. Feed with a water-soluble plant food such as Miracle-Gro Water Soluble Tomato Plant Food, following package directions.

PESTS: The most common diseases are anthracnose, early blight, septoria leaf spot, tobacco mosaic virus, fusarium wilt, and verticillium wilt. Look for disease-resistant varieties. Tomatoes suffer from numerous physiological disorders caused by environmental stress. Moisture extremes cause blossom-end rot. Skin cracking happens when hot rainy periods follow dry spells. Temperature extremes lead to blossom drop. Sunscald results from overexposure to the sun on one side of the fruit.

Handpick and destroy Japanese beetles or hornworms. Control fruitworms and stinkbugs with a labeled insecticide.

Harvest

Begin picking tomatoes when they reach full size and color. Tomatoes will continue ripening off the plant, even in the dark. The pigments that give fruits their distinctive color do not develop well in high temperatures, so tomatoes harvested during midsummer may be more yellow than when picked in cooler weather.

Pick any fruits remaining on the vine at the first predicted autumn frost. Fruits that have a hint of yellow often continue to ripen if held in a dark, warm location. Store them in single layers between sheets of newspaper.

Notes

< **47** >

This map of climate zones helps you select plants for your garden that will survive a typical winter in your region. The United States Department of Agriculture (USDA) developed the map, basing the zones on the lowest recorded temperatures across North America. Zone 1 is the coldest area and Zone 11 is the warmest.

Plants are classified by the coldest temperature and zone they can endure. For example, plants hardy to Zone 6 survive where winter temperatures drop to –10° F. Those hardy to Zone 8 die long before it's that cold. These plants may grow in colder regions but must be replaced each year. Plants rated for a range of hardiness zones can usually survive winter in the coldest region as well as tolerate the summer heat of the warmest one.

To find your hardiness zone, note the approximate location of your community on the map, then match the color band marking that area to the key.

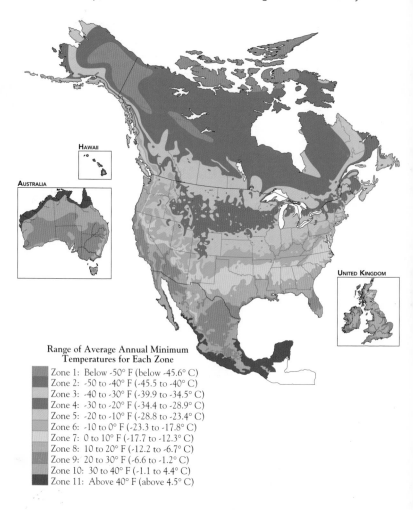

Range of Average Annual Minimum Temperatures for Each Zone

Zone 1: Below -50° F (below -45.6° C)
Zone 2: -50 to -40° F (-45.5 to -40° C)
Zone 3: -40 to -30° F (-39.9 to -34.5° C)
Zone 4: -30 to -20° F (-34.4 to -28.9° C)
Zone 5: -20 to -10° F (-28.8 to -23.4° C)
Zone 6: -10 to 0° F (-23.3 to -17.8° C)
Zone 7: 0 to 10° F (-17.7 to -12.3° C)
Zone 8: 10 to 20° F (-12.2 to -6.7° C)
Zone 9: 20 to 30° F (-6.6 to -1.2° C)
Zone 10: 30 to 40° F (-1.1 to 4.4° C)
Zone 11: Above 40° F (above 4.5° C)